OVERCOMING

By Steven P. Kaelin

Kaelin Books
Salt Lake City, Utah

Published in Salt Lake City, Utah, by Kaelin Books

Library of Congress Cataloging-in-Publication Data

Kaelin, Steven P., 1952-
Overcoming / by Steven P. Kaelin
p. cm.
ISBN 0-9650754-0-0
1. Overcoming Obstacles–Inspirational thoughts and stories

To Susan, Catherine & Jane.

For All We Have Overcome To Find Each Other.

INTRODUCTION

OVER the past 20 years, I have spent much of my professional career working with children and families. Many have faced overwhelming odds and obstacles with courage, faith, and hope. I am always amazed how resilient children and parents can be when faced with tremendous setbacks and defeats.

This book evolved as I looked for inspirational stories for parents who love and care for children who have been seriously abused and neglected. In the process,

I discovered a collection of heroic examples that teach about the challenges of life and the great potential for people to rise above negative circumstances.

This book is a gift of hope. It is a reminder that everyone has the ability to turn seeming disaster into enduring victory. The measure of greatness is not so much in what people have achieved, but what they have Overcome.

Steven P. Kaelin

Acknowledgments

A cry for help in the early hours of the morning brought three great souls to my rescue. I am indebted to them eternally–Bob, Dan, Georgia.

Three other great souls inspire me to live courageously, when all seems lost–Susan, Catherine, Jane.

And to my parents and four brothers–Thanks. It is nice to have you at my side for the entire ride.

OVERCOMING

"The human soul, beaten down, overwhelmed, faced by complete failure and ruin, can still rise up against unbearable odds and triumph."

Harold Russell

"Adversity causes some men to break; others to break records."

William A. Ward

"If you have the determination, you can come back from failure and succeed."

Eddie Rickenbacker

Aesop, a Greek fabulist. He created many short stories about animals, which taught about human virtues and follies. These fables have been passed down for generations.

Aesop (620 B.C. - 560 B.C.)

Aesop was a slave. He was physically deformed. He recounted his beautiful fables amid the dust and decadence of ancient streets and on doorsteps of unimpressed listeners.

Alcott, American author. She is known for her books for children – *Little Women*, *An Old-Fashioned Girl*, *Little Men*, *Jo's Boys*, *Flower Fables*, etc.

Louisa May Alcott (1832 - 1888)

Alcott was born into an extremely poor family. As a teenager, she became responsible for supporting her family financially. She often suffered from nightmares and hallucinations.

When asked to write a book for girls, she felt that she couldn't because it wasn't her type of writing.

Andersen, Danish author. He wrote many classic fairy tales for children, including *The Emperor's New Clothes*, *The Little Match Girl*, *The Ugly Duckling*, *Thumbelina*, *The Little Mermaid*, *The Constant Tin Soldier*, etc.

Hans Christian Andersen (1805 - 1875)

Andersen was dyslexic. He was also a sensitive and highly active boy with a vivid imagination. He disliked school and often stayed home to "frivolously" spend his day creating strange creatures and playing with the toy theatre he built for himself. When he was eleven years old, his father died. At this young age, Andersen traveled to Copenhagen, Denmark, to become a writer.

He never thought much of his fairy tales. He wrote them for his own entertainment.

Anderson, American short story writer and novelist. He wrote about life in the Midwest and achieved fame with such novels as *Beyond Desire*, *Dark Laughter*, and *Winesburg, Ohio*.

Sherwood Anderson (1876 - 1941)

Anderson was late to school thirty-two times one semester. His teachers did not consider him to have much academic potential, so he was permitted to stay home permanently to help his mother.

Aristotle, Greek philosopher. He was a disciple of Plato for nineteen years. He taught in Athens and developed theories of metaphysics and ethics. His works included *De Anima*, *Metaphysics* and *Nicomachean Ethics*.

Aristotle (384 B.C. - 322 B.C.)

Aristotle stuttered when he spoke.

Audubon, American artist and ornithologist. He accurately and beautifully painted all of the species of birds in the U.S. known in the early 19th Century.

John Audubon (1785 - 1851)

Audubon was born to unmarried parents and was raised by his stepmother. His business ventures and investments constantly failed. He once opened a store in Kentucky but spent so much time walking and hiking in the woods, observing birds and other wildlife, that his business failed.

Audubon had no formal training in science. His paintings of birds initially met with little success in the U.S. and had to be sent to Europe before they were published.

Beethoven, German composer, virtuoso pianist, master of orchestral form. He wrote some of the most beautiful and noble music the world has known including, *Eroica*, *Moonlight Sonata*, *Pathetique*, *Battle Symphony*, *Symphony No. 9*, etc.

Ludwig van Beethoven (1770 - 1827)

Beethoven was an abused child. His father would drag him out of bed late at night to make him practice and severely beat him when he made mistakes. His father was an alcoholic. His family lived in poverty.

Beethoven did not do well as a student of Haydn. He was deaf most of his adult life. He suffered constantly from chronic ear inflammations, permanent buzzing and earaches, as well as extreme depressions and uncontrollable sorrow. He was near- sighted, very sensitive about his perceived ugliness, and never married. He lived from day-to-day, often deprived of basic necessities. He often received no payment for his musical masterpieces. He lived alone and was called "unfeeling." He never heard some of his greatest works.

Buck, American novelist. She was a prolific writer. Author of *The Good Earth*, *Sons*, *The Mother*, *A House Divided*, and *Dragon Seed*. She was awarded the Nobel Prize in literature in 1938.

Pearl Buck (1892 - 1973)

Pearl Buck's manuscript for *The Good Earth* was rejected fourteen times before it was eventually published.

Burns, Scottish poet and songwriter. He wrote numerous poems, approximately three hundred songs, including *Auld Lang Syne*, *Comin' Thro' the Rye*.

Robert Burns (1759 - 1796)

Burns lived in poverty his entire life. This hard, dreary life made him sickly. In love, he was rejected and bitterly disappointed.

Burr, Vice President of the U.S. Revolutionary War Veteran and Senator from New York.

Aaron Burr (1756 - 1836)

Burr's parents died when he was three years old. He was raised by an uncle. He was continually opposed and attacked politically and was considered a social outcast.

Byron, English romantic poet.

Lord Byron (1788 - 1824)

Lord Byron was physically handicapped with a club foot. As a child, he suffered poverty and was abused by his unstable mother.

Carlyle, Scottish philosopher, critic and historian.

Thomas Carlyle (1795 - 1881)

Carlyle was the oldest of nine children. He struggled financially most of his life. He endured many years of misery and obscurity. After working on the original manuscript of the *History of the French Revolution* for several years, it was accidentally destroyed in a fire. He had to rewrite the extensive three volume manuscript.

Carroll, English mathematician, photographer and novelist. He wrote the popular children's classics, *Alice's Adventures in Wonderland* and *Through the Looking-Glass*.

Lewis Carroll (1832 - 1898)

Carroll was a very shy and timid man. He did not make friends easily. He sometimes stammered when he spoke and lectured. Carroll's primary vocation was a university professor of mathematics. He thought it undignified for a university professor to write stories for children. He did not want anyone to know that he had written children's books and initially never thought of publishing his childish adventure stories.

Carver, American agricultural chemist and scientist. He derived more than three hundred products from peanuts, sweet potatoes, and soy beans. He was the head of the Department of Agriculture at Tuskegee Institute in Alabama.

George Washington Carver (1864 - 1943)

Carver was born a slave. His father was killed before George was born. When he was six weeks old, he was kidnapped and separated from his mother by nightriders. As a child, he was sickly and stammered badly when he talked. He was raised in extreme poverty. He was not allowed to attend school and did not learn to read until he was nearly an adult.

Cervantes, Spanish novelist, poet, and dramatist. His most famous work is *Don Quixote de la Mancha*.

Miguel de Cervantes (1547 - 1616)

Cervantes wrote much of the book *Don Quixote* while in prison. Throughout most of his life, he struggled financially. He could not support himself through writing. He never rose above the rank of private in his chosen career as a professional soldier. He lost a hand while serving in the Army. When he was twenty-eight years old, he was captured and held as a slave in Algiers for five years.

Cézanne, French painter. He had one of the most important influences on twentieth century art.

Paul Cézanne (1839 - 1906)

Cézanne was rejected by the Ecole des Beaux Arts when he applied for admission.

Chaplin, English actor and filmmaker. Widely accepted as the greatest comedian of the silent era and a brilliant mime. He was knighted in 1975.

Charlie Chaplin (1889 - 1977)

Chaplin was born and raised in the slums of London. His parents separated when he was two years old. He was placed in an orphanage from age five to seven. In the orphanage, he never had enough to eat. He was flogged and put in solitary confinement for small infractions. Chaplin's father died from alcoholism and his mother was mentally ill. At times, she did not recognize her own son.

Charles, singer and pianist. He has had a very successful blues and popular singing career. His first big hit song, *I Got a Woman* was in 1955. He has won ten Grammy Awards.

Ray Charles (1932 -)

Ray Charles was abandoned by his father at a very young age. When Ray was five years old, he watched his four year old brother drown in a large wash tub. He tried to pull his brother out but he was too small to help.

Ray became blind at age six. His right eye was surgically removed when he was seven years old. His mother died from a heart attack when he was fourteen years old.

At age sixteen, Ray auditioned for a nationally acclaimed big band. The band leader told him, "Sorry kid, you ain't good enough. You don't got what it takes."

Chávez, American labor leader. He organized the National Farm Workers Association and led a successful national boycott.

César Chávez (1927 - 1993)

Chávez's parents were illiterate migrant farm workers. His family moved a great deal and eventually settled in California. César attended more than thirty grammar schools before dropping out of school when he was twelve years old.

Chekhov, Russian dramatist. His most famous works include *The Cherry Orchard*, *The Three Sisters*, and *The Seagull*.

Anton Chekhov (1860 - 1904)

Chekhov's father was cruel and had a bad temper. He beat Anton and overworked him in his store. Anton's father was hated by his family. Anton was a poor student. He failed his secondary graduation exams twice.

Chopin, French/Polish composer and pianist. He is considered one of the greatest composers. He is best known for his ballads, etudes, nocturnes, waltzes, and preludes.

Frédéric Chopin (1810 - 1849)

Chopin died before he was forty years old. He was in bad health throughout his life. His health was worsened by his constant activity and drive.

Churchill, English Prime Minister and author.

Sir Winston Churchill (1874 - 1965)

Churchill was born two months premature. He hated school and failed the entrance exams to the Royal Military College at Sandhurst three times before he got accepted. His parents were rejecting, remote, and emotionally distant. When he was younger, he spoke with a lisp. Later he had a slight problem in pronouncing the letter "S". His father considered him lacking in intelligence and thought the only potential his son had was to be a soldier in the Army.

He had few friends growing up and often got low grades. A dancing teacher once described Winston as "the naughtiest boy in the class, possibly the naughtiest boy in the world." Churchill's initial warnings about the Nazi's were criticized and ignored.

Cody, American frontiersman, scout, and entertainer. He served as a scout during the Civil War. He produced the Wild West show which also included Annie Oakley and Chief Sitting Bull.

Buffalo Bill Cody (1846 - 1917)

Cody's father died when Cody was eleven years old. Buffalo Bill left school and joined a wagon train after he seriously injured another child, who wrecked the playhouse Bill and a friend were making.

Columbus, Italian explorer, discoverer of America. He made four voyages to the New World.

Christopher Columbus (1451 - 1506)

Columbus was unable to get help from the King of Portugal for his voyage. He eventually received three small ships and crews comprised of criminals and undesirables. Not all of his voyages to the New World were successful. He endured periods of hardship, imprisonment, sickness, doubts and mutinies. He died in poverty.

Confucius, Chinese founder of Confucianism.

Confucius (551 B.C. - 479 B.C.)

Confucius was forced to leave his home because of the jealousy of the ruler and dishonesty of officials. He was homeless for thirty years, wandering throughout China, never finding support for his teachings. Many of his writings were lost.

Conrad, Polish/British novelist. His novels dealt with psychological conflicts that people confront in extreme and difficult situations. His famous works include *Lord Jim*, *The Heart of Darkness*, *Nostromo*, *Victory*, etc.

Joseph Conrad (1857 - 1924)

Conrad watched his parents die painful and lingering deaths. His mother died when he was seven years old. His father was exiled to Siberia and died when Joseph was twelve years old.

Curie, Polish physicist. She discovered radium and polonium. She received the Nobel Prize in 1903 and 1911.

Marie Curie (1867 - 1934)

Curie grew up in poverty. Her mother died from tuberculosis when Marie was ten years old. Marie was always a serious and compulsive student and worker. She had two nervous breakdowns before ever achieving success.

Curie worked for many years in a cold, dilapidated, leaky shed, which no one else would use. Her scientific apparatus was primitive and inadequate due to a lack of funds. She often went without sleep and sufficient food for long periods of time. After the 487th experiment had failed, her husband, Pierre, exclaimed in despair, "It will never be done, maybe in a hundred years but never in our day."

Dali, Spanish artist. He was an influential and popular surrealistic painter. His paintings are displayed in major museums throughout the world.

Salvador Dali (1904 - 1989)

Dali was given the same name as his older brother, who died at age seven from meningitis. Salvador was born three years after his brother's death and was treated by his parents as if he were the deceased brother. Unable to live up to his parent's expectations and memories of his brother, Salvador became hyperactive and aggressive. As a teenager, he was so eccentric in his appearance and behavior that children threw rocks at him when he left his house. He was expelled from school when he refused to let teachers grade his art work.

Defoe, English journalist and novelist. His books include *Robinson Crusoe*, *Moll Flanders*, and *Roxana*.

Daniel Defoe (1660 - 1731)

Daniel Defoe wrote *Robinson Crusoe* when he was nearly sixty years old. At the time, he was very poor and was close to being sent to debtors prison. Defoe worked at many different occupations throughout his life. Publishers were very hesitant to publish *Robinson Crusoe* because it had a new and unfamiliar prose-fiction style.

Degas, French painter and sculptor. His works are now in major museums throughout the world.

Edgar Degas (1834 - 1917)

Degas had only one painting bought by an art museum during his lifetime. The work was entitled, *The Cotton Exchange at New Orleans*.

Dickens, English author. His famous works include *A Christmas Carol*, *David Copperfield*, *A Tale of Two Cities*, and *Great Expectations*.

Charles Dickens (1812 - 1870)

When Charles was nine years old, his family fell into serious financial difficulties. At age ten, he was forced to work in a squalid factory. He lived alone while his father was in debtor's prison.

Dickinson, American poet. She is recognized as one of the outstanding poets from the U.S.

Emily Dickinson (1830 - 1886)

Dickinson was extremely shy and fearful of strangers. Her mother was very sickly and needed constant attention from Emily. Emily lived in her parent's home her entire life and hardly ever went out.

Dickinson wrote approximately 1,800 poems but only seven poems were published in her lifetime. More than a thousand poems were found in her dresser drawers after she died.

Dietrich, American film star and singer. Her notable films include, *The Blue Angel*, *Blonde Venus*, *Destry Rides Again*, *Rancho Notorious*.

Marlene Dietrich (1902 - 1992)

Dietrich studied to be a violinist. She developed a tumor on her right wrist, which ended the opportunities for a career in music.

Dodge, American editor and author. She edited a children's magazine, *St. Nicholas* and wrote the classic *Hans Brinker, or the Silver Skates*.

Mary Elizabeth Mapes Dodge (1831 - 1905)

Mary Dodge began writing to earn a living after she was widowed with two young boys. Initially no publisher was interested in her book *Hans Brinker, or The Silver Skates*.

Doyle, English author. His famous works include, *Adventures of Sherlock Holmes*, *The Memories of Sherlock Holmes*, *A Study in Scarlet*.

Conan Doyle (1859 - 1930)

Conan Doyle was not a very successful physician in England. He wrote detective stories as a way to supplement his income. He did not consider these stories to be great works of literature. He preferred to write historical novels.

Eddy, founder of the Christian Science Church. Her book, *Science and Health* explains the Christian Science system for physical and mental healing.

Mary Baker Eddy (1821 - 1910)

As a child, Mary Baker Eddy suffered from unusual illnesses in which she had attacks of anger, hysteria and acute pains in her back. During these attacks, she would fall on the floor, pound her feet and go into an unconscious state. She also frequently heard voices and had difficulty attending school. Eddy had seizures and hallucinations throughout most of her life. An injured spine, at age forty-five, and subsequent "faith healing" led to her establishing a new religious society.

Edison, American inventor. He is known as the most productive inventor of his time. He received over one thousand patents, including an electronic vote recorder, telegraph transmitters and receivers, phonograph, telephone transmitters, incandescent lamp, mimeograph, dictating machines, motion picture cameras, projector, battery.

Thomas Edison (1847 - 1931)

Edison had very little formal education. He was dyslexic, a daydreamer and had a hearing impairment. He was taken out of school when he was in the first grade. He never attended school again. He was publicly beaten by his father, after setting fire to the barn. He began working at age seven.

Edison was considered an odd child, who was continually experimenting. He once tried to hatch eggs by sitting on them. His experiments also blew up a telegraph station and derailed a train. He almost killed a friend by pumping gas into his lungs to see if he would float.

Edison failed more than ten thousand times before he successfully invented the incandescent light bulb.

He once stated: "My father thought I was stupid, and I almost decided I must be a dunce."

Einstein, German/American physicist. He was awarded the Nobel Prize in 1921. After World War II, he was devoted to working for peace. Element 99 (Einsteinium) is named after him.

Albert Einstein (1879 - 1955)

Einstein was an unknown patent clerk in Bern, Switzerland, when at age twenty-six he published the *Theory of Relativity*.

As a child, teachers labeled Albert as mentally slow, unsociable and lost in foolish dreams. Other students nicknamed him Vater Langweil - Father Bore. His father was often annoyed by his eccentricities and preoccupation with self-centered activities.

When Einstein first applied to Zurich Polytechnic Academy, he failed the entrance exams. After he received a teaching certificate in math and physics, he was not able to find a teaching job in Germany because he was Jewish.

Erikson, American psychoanalyst. Boston's first child analyst. He extended Freud's theories to adolescence and adulthood. He created the term "identity crisis." Author of the classic psychological theory and work *Childhood and Society*.

Erik Erikson (1902 - 1994)

Erikson's parents separated before his birth. His mother remarried and he was adopted by his stepfather. Erik was born in Germany. His biological parents were Danish and his adoptive father was Jewish. Because of this diversity, as he was growing up, he felt he had no strong cultural or ethnic identity. He also disliked school and rebelled against its rules and structure. At age twenty-five, he was more interested in art than psychology.

Though Erikson was a popular professor at Harvard, he had no academic degrees.

Fermi, Italian physicist. He studied atomic energy and structure. He received the Nobel Prize in 1938.

Enrico Fermi (1901 - 1954)

Enrico was bored and restless in school. He did not feel very challenged in his schoolwork. He was almost expelled from high school for leading a "stink bomb" attack on the teachers.

Foster, American composer and songwriter. He wrote over two hundred songs, many musical classics including, *Oh Susanna*, *Camptown Races*, *Old Folks at Home*, *My Old Kentucky Home*, etc.

Stephen Foster (1826 - 1864)

Stephen was very absent-minded. He frequently walked in public without acknowledging anyone. He was not formally trained in music and was an extremely poor businessman. As a result of financial problems, at age thirty-one, Foster sold all rights to his future songs to his publishers for about $1,900. The profits from his songs went largely to performers and publishers. Despite the immense popularity of his songs, in the earlier years of his life, he died in poverty and obscurity.

Franklin, American inventor, diplomat, and statesman.

Benjamin Franklin (1706 - 1790)

Franklin had only two years of formal education. He attended school from age eight to ten. He was the youngest of fifteen children.

Fulton, American inventor and engineer. His main interest was in navigation. He is best known for the Clermont, which pioneered the use of steamboats for carrying freight and passengers.

Robert Fulton (1765 - 1815)

Fulton was a portrait painter by profession. He was also an apprenticed jeweler.

Fulton's first steamboat was ridiculed and called "Fulton's Folly." While living in Paris, he built a submarine and offered it to Napoleon. Napoleon refused the offer.

Galileo, Italian scientist, professor, astronomer. He invented the telescope and studied laws of motion.

Galileo (1564 - 1642)

Galileo's father called his son an absent-minded little stargazer who saw strange visions and heard uncanny sounds. He failed as a medical student.

Galileo's theories were continually in conflict with the religious dogmas of his day. He was carefully watched and was forced by the inquisition to recant statements. He was also forbidden to publish books and articles.

Galileo's third and final book was written while he was in prison. He wrote secretly and had to smuggle it out of prison for publication in Holland. He never saw the printed copy of this book because he went blind in prison. He enjoyed holding this book. Of this book, he stated, "I esteem this the most of all my works. It is the outcome of my extreme agony."

Gandhi, Indian leader. He was known as the "Great Lord." His leadership was responsible for winning independence for India.

Mohandas K. Gandhi (1869 - 1948)

Gandhi was never elected to a political office. He lived simply and without many modern conveniences. His home did not have electric lights, running water, or a telephone. He did not have a car. He did not own property.

Goethe, German poet, dramatist, scientist and court official.

Goethe [Johann Wolfgang von]
(1749 - 1832)

It took Goethe sixty years to write *Faust*. He started at age twenty-three and finished at eighty-three. During his life, he was a lawyer, botanist, politician, civil servant, physicist, zoologist, painter, and theatre manager.

Golding, English novelist. His works include, *Lord of the Flies*, *The Inheritors*, *The Spire*, *Darkness Visible*, and *A Moving Target*.

William Golding (1911 - 1993)

Golding's novel, *Lord of the Flies*, was rejected twenty-one times before it was published.

Gorky, Russian dramatist and writer. His works include *The Lower Depths*, *Mother*, *The Enemies*.

Maxim Gorky [Alexei Peshkov]
(1868 - 1936)

Alexei's father died of cholera when Alexei was four years old. He was raised by quarreling and abusive grandparents, who often beat him until he was unconscious. Peshkov was forced to leave home at age ten to find work. At age nineteen, he was so troubled and burdened by struggles, he attempted suicide. He later gave himself a new name - Maxim Gorky, "Man of Bitterness."

Grant, American commander of the Union Forces during the Civil War and the eighteenth President of the United States.

Ulysses S. Grant (1822 - 1885)

Grant was forced to resign from the Army at age thirty-two, because of alcoholism. He failed at farming and real estate, so he went back to work at his father's tanning shop. After the Civil War broke out, and when he was thirty-nine years old, he was given the command of a volunteer regiment in Illinois. Seven years later, he was President of the United States.

Grieg, Norwegian composer. He was called the "Chopin of the North."

Edward Grieg (1843 - 1907)

At age fifteen, Grieg became seriously ill with pleurisy. This illness permanently damaged his lungs, weakened his health, and reduced his physical energy and stamina. Grieg did not plan to become a musician. As a child, he was a dreamer and rebellious at school. He was labeled lazy and stupid. He hated school. He was ridiculed by his teachers and enjoyed getting kicked out of school. He stated, "School developed in me nothing but what was evil and left the good untouched." At age twenty-two, the parents of his fiancée stated, "He is nothing, he has nothing and makes music no one wants to hear." Throughout most of his life, his musical efforts were often opposed or met with indifference.

Handel, German composer. He is regarded as the greatest composer of the Baroque period. He completed forty-six operas, thirty-two oratorios, more than one hundred large vocal works, numerous dramatic pieces, many solo instrumentals and orchestral compositions. Of him Beethoven stated, "To him I bend the knee, for Handel is the greatest, ablest composer that ever lived."

George Frideric Handel (1685 - 1759)

Handel's father hated music and strongly opposed his son's musical career. He considered music self-indulgence and a sign of weakness. Young Handel smuggled a piano into the attic of their house. He deadened the sound with strips of cloth around the strings so he could practice without his father hearing.

At age forty-five, Handel lost his popularity and was faced with disgrace and debtors prison. He lost his sight six years before he died. During this time, he gave organ concerts and conducted performances of his oratorios. The *Messiah* was not very successful when it was first introduced in London. It was considered sacrilegious.

Haydn, Austrian composer. One of the greatest composers of the classical period. He wrote 104 symphonies.

Franz Joseph Haydn (1732 - 1809)

Haydn was raised by his uncle who was an insensitive disciplinarian. Young Joseph was mentally and physically abused and neglected. As a youngster, he was self-conscious and awkward. He was temperamental and had rapidly shifting moods. He was rejected, harassed and treated with contempt by other children.

Haydn was unhappily married. He fought frequently with his wife. He was described as an unhappy man, extremely lonely, with continual sadness in his eyes.

Hawthorne, American writer. His famous works include *The Scarlet Letter*, *The House of Seven Gables*, *The Snow Image* and *Other Twice-Told Tales*.

Nathaniel Hawthorne (1804 - 1864)

Hawthorne became crippled after an accident when he was a young boy. As a child, he was reticent, aloof and had very few friends. Hawthorne was a neglected and emotionally deprived child. Most of his childhood was spent in solitude.

Hawthorne initially worked in a customs house to earn a living. He hated this job. He felt he was a failure because he could not earn enough to support his family or sell his writings.

At age forty-five, he was fired from his job at the customs house. During this time, while writing the *Scarlet Letter*, he became sick and despondent. He felt he could no longer write and would never be a popular writer.

Hemingway, American author. His works include, *The Sun Also Rises*, *A Farewell to Arms*, *For Whom the Bell Tolls*, *The Old Man & The Sea*. He received the Nobel Prize for literature in 1954.

Earnest Hemingway (1899 - 1961)

Hemingway was very accident prone. His eyesight was poor. He shattered his nose at age fourteen. Later in life, he had 227 steel splinters in his right leg. He had gunshot wounds in both hands, feet, and knees. He had six severe head injuries, six broken ribs, and ten brain concussions.

Henry, American patriot, orator, and statesman.

Patrick Henry (1736 - 1799)

Patrick was a very lazy youngster. He preferred hunting and fishing to going to school. He skipped school often to go exploring in the woods.

In court, he once mistakenly argued the opposition's position. When told of his mistake, he persuasively answered all of his own arguments and won the judgment in favor of his client.

He was the father of seventeen children.

Hesse, German novelist and poet. His works include, *Demian*, *Siddhartha*, *Steppenwolf*, *Narcissus and Goldmund*, and *The Glass Bead Game*.

Herman Hesse (1877 - 1962)

Hesse was such a problem child, at age six his mother seriously considered placing him in a corrective institution.

He really hated school and was very rebellious. At age fifteen, he attempted suicide. He later ran away from a theological school.

Heyerdahl, Norwegian ethnologist. He wrote numerous books about his travels and explorations on the balsa raft, *Kon Tiki* and the papyrus boat, *Ra II*.

Thor Heyerdahl (1914 -   )

As a child, Heyerdahl was sickly and was not able to attend school regularly because of health problems.

Hoover, Thirty-first President of the United States.

Herbert Hoover (1874 - 1964)

Hoover was orphaned at the age of ten. He was separated from his siblings and lived with various aunts and uncles. A single school teacher wanted to adopt him but his relatives were opposed to this arrangement.

Hugo, French poet, dramatist, novelist. His works include, *Notre Dame de Paris*, *Les Miserables*.

Victor Hugo (1802 - 1885)

Hugo lived in exile for over twenty years.

Hussein, King of Jordan.

King Hussein I (1935 -)

Hussein's mother was mentally ill. His father also had sudden psychotic episodes in which he became violent and dangerous.

Jackson, Seventh President of the United States.

Andrew Jackson (1767 - 1845)

Jackson was from a poor family. He was raised on the frontier with little education. He was orphaned at age thirteen. At this age, he joined the colonies fight for independence and was soon captured by the British. His face was scarred when an officer hit him with his sabre for refusing to polish the officer's boots.

Jefferson, Third President of the United States.

Thomas Jefferson (1743 - 1826)

Jefferson suffered from excruciating migraine headaches.

Joan of Arc, national heroine of France. Canonized by the Roman Catholic Church, she was declared a Saint in 1920.

Joan of Arc (1412 - 1431)

Throughout her childhood, Joan of Arc was extremely happy and healthy. At age thirteen, she began to hear voices and felt that she would be an instrument in God's hands to free France from British rule. When she set out to accomplish her inspired mission, she was a young adolescent with no experience in military operations or politics.

Keats, English poet. Important poems include, *To a Nightingale*, *Ode on a Grecian Urn*, *Endymion*.

John Keats (1795 - 1821)

Keats was the son of a stable keeper. He developed problems with his throat, as a result of exposure and living in open conditions. He later developed tuberculosis. Keats studied medicine but gave up his medical career to write poetry. His works were often met with harsh critical reviews. He died at the age of twenty-six.

Keller, American author and social worker. She achieved distinction as a lecturer and scholar. She received a degree from Radcliffe College and mastered several languages.

She once stated, "I thank God for my handicaps, for through them I have found myself, my work, and my God."

Helen Keller (1880 - 1968)

Keller became blind and deaf after an illness when she was almost two years old. Her parents were devastated by her condition. They did not know how to cope with Helen's physical and behavioral problems until Anne Sullivan was hired to teach and care for their daughter.

Kennedy, Thirty-fifth President of the United States. First Roman Catholic ever elected to the Presidency.

John F. Kennedy (1917 - 1963)

When Kennedy was distinguished as "most likely to succeed" in his class at Choate in 1935, he asked a friend, "Most likely to succeed at what?" At Harvard, he was an average student. He lost his older brother during WWII. His brother was killed during a bombing mission in Germany.

Kennedy's first political victory in the eleventh congressional district was won by sheer determination. He campaigned door-to-door from dawn until midnight. Back pain (from his injury in WWII) often forced him to use crutches as he walked the stairs of three story tenement buildings. His days without pain were rare. He was determined to live with the pain and a minimum of medication. He was silent in his suffering.

King, American clergyman and civil rights leader. Youngest person ever to receive the Nobel Prize.

Martin Luther King, Jr. (1929 - 1968)

As a boy, King rebelled against religion. For a time, he was agnostic. He had no plans to go into the ministry when he entered college at age fifteen. He had planned to be a doctor.

King endured criticism and abuse from critics and former friends. At thirty-eight, he had been jailed nineteen times. He once stated, "I will rot in jail before I make a butchery of my conscience."

Lamb, English poet and essayist.

Charles Lamb (1775 - 1834)

Lamb had an incurable stuttering problem. His speech kept him from professions in the church and university. When he was twenty-one years old, his sister went insane and stabbed his mother to death. Lamb devoted the rest of his life to caring for his mentally ill sister. He worked for thirty-three years as a bookkeeper. He called his accounting books his true works.

Lawrence, English author and soldier, known as Lawrence of Arabia.

T.E. Lawrence (1888 - 1935)

After discovering in his late teens that he and his four brothers were born to unmarried parents, he ran away from his upper-middle-class home and enlisted as a private in The Royal Artillery. He rejected both of his parents. He felt they were both unfit to be his parents.

Leakey, English archeologist and anthropologist.

Louis Leakey (1903 - 1972)

Leakey suffered a blow to his head while playing rugby in college. As a result of this injury, he suffered severe headaches, epileptic seizures and memory loss.

For health reasons, it was recommended that he take a break from school and spend more time in the open air. During his recovery, he spent eight months on a dinosaur excavation. This experience lead to his future professional interests and success.

Lincoln, Sixteenth President of the United States.

Abraham Lincoln (1809 - 1865)

Lincoln was a homely backwoods man. He was born in a log cabin. His mother died when he was nine years old. His formal education totalled less than a year. His primary teachers were poverty, work and solitude. Lincoln studied law in his spare time, while running a general store. His earnings as a lawyer at their highest were very meager. Lincoln had a very difficult marriage and grieved the loss of two young children. He led this country during a time of bitter conflict and alienation.

Lindberg, American author. Her works include, *Gift from the Sea*, *The Unicorn*, *Dearly Beloved*, *North to the Orient*.

Anne Morrow Lindberg (1907 -   )

Anne was a very shy child. She felt inferior to her older sister. Her aviator husband was also quite shy. Her first child was kidnapped and murdered.

London, American writer. His books include, *Call of the Wild*, *Martin Eden*, and *John Barleycorn*.

Jack London (1876 - 1916)

London was never acknowledged or supported by his father. His mother made two attempts at suicide when she was pregnant with Jack. She first took an overdose of opium, later she shot herself with a revolver.

London grew up in the slums of Oakland, California. He began working fourteen hours a day in a cannery when he was thirteen years old. He was a juvenile delinquent and was involved in petty crimes. He was described as a "methodical and stubborn boy with a private world which he defended fiercely." Jack once stated, "I have never had a boyhood and I seem to be hunting for that lost boyhood."

Before the age of twenty-five, London had been a fisherman, college student, hobo and prospector.

Luther, German leader of the Protestant reformation. He wrote hymns, catechisms and translated the New Testament into German.

Martin Luther (1483 - 1546)

Luther was the son of a peasant. To support himself while attending the university in Germany, he sang in the streets.

Luther was excommunicated from the Catholic Church after writing a protest against the practice of accepting money to forgive sins.

Magellan, Portuguese and Spanish explorer. He organized the first expedition to go around the world.

Ferdinand Magellan (1480 - 1521)

Magellan had to eat leather and rats to survive the voyage that proved the earth is round. He also endured severe storms, mutiny and sickness.

Mahler, Austrian composer and conductor of the Romantic period.

Gustav Mahler (1860 - 1911)

Five of Mahler's brothers and sisters died in childhood from diphtheria. Mahler was particularly close to another brother, who died at age twelve, after a long illness. Mahler's oldest sister died from a brain tumor, after a brief and unhappy marriage. Another sister was a hypochondriac and was preoccupied with delusions regarding death. Another brother was a forger and another brother committed suicide, depressed over his mediocrity as a musician.

Marciano, American professional boxer. Undefeated World Heavyweight Champion from 1952-1956. He was the only heavyweight champion to retire undefeated. He won forty-three of his forty-nine bouts by knockout.

Rocky Marciano (1923 - 1969)

Growing up, Rocky dreamed of being a major league baseball player. He was dropped from the Chicago Cubs after a two week tryout.

When Rocky started professional boxing at age twenty-five, he was considered too old, too small and too clumsy. His arms were short and his legs too big. He threw wild punches. He fought off balance and he had no left hook. He was told he would never make it as a professional boxer.

Milton, English poet. His works include *L'Allegro*, *Il Penseroso*, *Comus*, *Lycidas*, *Samson Agonistes*.

John Milton (1608 - 1674)

Milton went blind at the age of forty-four. He was blind for twenty-two years. During this time, his greatest poems, *Paradise Lost* and *Paradise Regained*, were dictated line-by-line to his daughters and friends. These enduring works were initially sold to the publisher for fifty dollars.

Monet, French impressionistic painter. He painted many seascapes, city scenes, and various views of the Seine River.

Claude Monet (1840 - 1926)

Monet was an extremely difficult child to manage at home and school. He was disrespectful, particularly in drawing classes and was truant from school.

Morse, American inventor. Developed the telegraph and Morse code. One of the founders of Vassar College.

Samuel F. B. Morse (1791 - 1872)

Morse was a successful portrait painter in New York. He founded the National Academy of Design. At age forty-two, Morse shifted his interests from art to science. He experimented for twelve years before developing a practical system for the telegraph. His telegraph invention was initially rejected by the United States and other foreign countries for over five years.

Naismith, American basketball pioneer. He originated the game of basketball, using two peach baskets and a soccer ball.

James Naismith (1861 - 1939)

Naismith was orphaned when his father and mother died from typhoid. Relatives helped him financially so he could go to college. They wanted him to be a minister but he took a job with the YMCA instead.

He worked with delinquent boys who didn't appreciate playing the popular indoor games of the time. This motivated Naismith to invent a new game - basketball.

Napoleon, general and Emperor of France. Military genius.

Napoleon [Bonaparte] (1769 - 1821)

Napoleon was so poor when he was attending school that he sold his watch and books for food. He rose from obscurity as a poor, insignificant officer to Emperor of France.

Newton, English scientist. Discoverer of law of gravitation, laws of motion, binomial theorem, and the basis of calculus.

Sir Isaac Newton (1642 - 1727)

Newton was a sickly child. He was born prematurely after his father's death. He wasn't expected to live. Newton did very poor academically as a youth. He was described as having an unruly temperament and unpredictable habits.

A great mathematician challenged all Europe's scientists to solve a certain problem and gave them a year to complete it. Newton solved the problem in one day.

Newton made some of his greatest discoveries while working at home during the eighteen months closure of Cambridge University during the Plague.

Nightingale, English nurse and hospital reformer. She devoted her life to the improvement of nursing and public health.

Florence Nightingale (1820 - 1910)

During Nightingale's time, nursing was considered an undesirable and disreputable occupation, particularly for wealthy English socialites. In spite of the strong objections of her family, Nightingale secretly trained to be a nurse. Caring for the sick became her life's work. She cared for injured soldiers during the Crimean War, lacking sufficient money and supplies.

Nijinsky, Russian dancer. One of the greatest male ballet dancers. He toured South America, Europe, and the United States performing *Prince Igor*, *Schéhérazade*, and *Pétrouchka*.

Vaslav Nijinsky (1890 - 1950)

Nijinsky was severely rejected by his peers. They refused to play with him or sit next to him at school. They often played cruel practical jokes on him, which sometimes seriously hurt him. One prank left him with a head injury and a crushed chest. He had to learn to walk again after a long recovery. His mother once planned a party and invited his classmates. She spent the last of what little money she had for the party. All of the children accepted the invitation but no one came to the party. Vaslav was devastated and cried uncontrollably.

Nin, American author. Her novels include, *Winter of Artifice*, *A Spy in the House of Love*. Extensive parts of her diaries and letters have also been published.

Anais Nin (1903 - 1977)

As a young girl, Anais was so shy people thought she was retarded. She often would hide under a big round table. When she was eleven years old, her father abandoned the family. At age fifteen, Anais dropped out of high school and worked as a model to help her family financially. Nin began writing in her diary when her father deserted the family. She used this as a way to communicate with her father, hoping he would someday read her entries when he returned. He never did.

Pasteur, French chemist and founder of microbiology, vaccination, pasteurization.

Louis Pasteur (1822 - 1895)

A school teacher once wrote of Pasteur, "He is the meekest, smallest, and least promising pupil in my class." Pasteur received mediocre grades in chemistry throughout college.

While Pasteur was investigating the silkworm epidemic, he worked eighteen hours a day. He had a paralyzing stroke and almost died. During his convalescence and recovery, he discovered the solution to the silkworm problem.

Pasteur was partially paralyzed when he first developed the process of pasteurization. His ideas and theories were often met with bitter and stubborn opposition. Malicious stories were spread about him and his work.

Peary, American arctic explorer. First man to stand on top of the world, 1909.

Robert E. Peary (1856 - 1920)

On his expedition to the North Pole, Peary and his company were continually troubled by blizzards, dense fogs and frostbite. He fought his way over one thousand miles of frozen land in spite of serious obstacles, accidents, and lack of vital supplies.

Peary's wife went with him on two trips to the Arctic. His daughter, Marie, was born in the Arctic Icelands.

Poe, American poet, writer and creator of the modern detective stories. His famous works are, *The Tell-Tale Heart*, *The Pit and the Pendulum*, *The Purloined Letter*, *The Raven*, *Annabel Lee*.

Edgar Allan Poe (1809 - 1849)

Poe's parents were traveling actors. They both died when he was two years old. Edgar's brother was taken in by paternal grandparents and his sister lived with close friends. Poe was raised by strict foster parents, who never legally adopted him and left him nothing when they died. His creative and impulsive nature clashed with their rigidness.

At age twenty-two, Poe was court-martialed and expelled from West Point. In college, he drank and gambled heavily. Poe endured poverty. He never found happiness and security in any relationship. He had a very difficult marriage. His wife had serious health problems. He had difficulty getting published. Despite his problems and disappointments, Poe continued to write. When he died at age forty, he was considered a failure by the literary community of his time.

Polo, first European traveler to cross the continent of Asia.

Marco Polo (1254 - 1324)

Polo was captured in a war with Genoa. While in prison, he dictated to a friend the story of his travels. These tales encouraged explorers to seek new routes in search for riches in the East. Columbus was among those who were inspired by Polo's travels.

Porter, American composer and lyricist. Despite his intense physical problems, Porter composed over 350 songs, 12 theatre shows, and 19 musicals after his riding accident.

Cole Porter (1891 - 1964)

Porter had over thirty-two operations on his legs. His legs were crushed in a horseback riding accident. He lived with extreme pain for the last twenty-seven years of his life. He was confined to a wheelchair and his right leg was later amputated. Porter also suffered from intense headaches.

He once stated that his mother's demands that he practice two hours every day had ruined his childhood.

Pulitzer, American journalist. He pioneered sensational journalism and founded the Pulitzer Prizes.

Joseph Pulitzer (1847 - 1911)

Pulitzer went blind at age forty.

Raleigh, English soldier, explorer, political figure, and author. Introduced the potato plant and tobacco from North America to England.

Sir Walter Raleigh (1552 - 1618)

Raleigh wrote the *History of the World* while he was in prison in the Tower of London for thirteen years.

Reich, Viennese psychologist who developed a system of psychoanalysis that concentrated on overall character structure.

Wilhelm Reich (1897 - 1957)

Reich carried guilt feelings about causing the death of his parents. After telling his father about his mother's infidelity, his mother committed suicide. Three years later, his father died from tuberculosis.

Rembrandt, Dutch painter and graphic artist. He had a life-long empathy and concern for the downtrodden and the poor.

Rembrandt (1606 - 1669)

Rembrandt was a simple man. He was very absentminded. He lived in poverty and continued his unique style of painting despite his lack of popularity and acceptance.

Rogers, American humorist. Remembered for his trick roping, humorous social criticisms, books and newspaper column.

Will Rogers (1879 - 1935)

Rogers was incorrigible at school and ran away from home. He was the youngest of a family of seven children and completed only the first four years of school.

Roosevelt E., First Lady, American reformer, humanitarian and writer. She worked for social causes. She raised a large family and helped her polio-stricken husband, Franklin, regain his strength.

U.S. Ambassador to the United Nations, she was described as the most influential woman of her time. "A passionate advocate for the weak and disadvantaged, an inspirational woman of compassion."

Eleanor Roosevelt (1884 - 1962)

Eleanor's mother died from diphtheria when Eleanor was eight years old. Her father was an alcoholic and at times suicidal. He died when Eleanor was ten years old. Eleanor felt that her mother never fully approved of her. She stated, "My mother was troubled by my lack of beauty." Her mother ridiculed her before guests and called her "granny." She didn't like her "homely" little daughter to touch her. Eleanor was shy, introverted, very conscious of her awkwardness. As a child, she wrote sad stories about lonely children who yearned for love.

Eleanor was raised by her grandmother, who was a strict disciplinarian and forced Eleanor to dress in old fashioned styles. She was shunned and ridiculed by other children because of her odd dress and ways.

Roosevelt F., Thirty-second President of the United States. He won a landslide victory when elected President in 1932. Regarding his attack of polio, Alden Hatch stated, "Without that tragic interlude, Roosevelt might well have become President, but not a great President."

Franklin D. Roosevelt (1882 - 1945)

Roosevelt was paralyzed by polio at the age of thirty-nine. He eventually gained partial use of his legs but he was crippled for the rest of his life. He needed braces and crutches to stand and could not dress without assistance. For three years, he received physical therapy to regain control of his body and to strengthen his legs. It took him seven years to make a political comeback after this crippling disease. He served as President of the United States for three terms during the Great Depression and World War II.

Roosevelt T., Twenty-sixth President of the United States.

Theodore Roosevelt (1858 - 1919)

Theodore Roosevelt was a very weak and sickly child. He was not well enough to attend school, so he was tutored at home. Roosevelt was blind in one eye. This was a result of a boxing match while he was serving in the Army.

Rubinstein, American pianist. He had the longest active concert career of any musician – more than seventy-five years.

Arthur Rubinstein (1886 - 1982)

Rubinstein, the youngest of seven children, was an unwanted child. Neither of Rubinstein's parents were musical. They never fully appreciated his incredible ability. This lack of musical appreciation created serious barriers between Rubinstein and his parents. When Rubinstein was ten years old, he was sent to live in Berlin with strangers. He became estranged from his parents.

Ruth, American baseball player. He hit 714 home runs, 60 homers in 1927, established a World Series record of consecutive scoreless innings as a pitcher and was elected to the Baseball Hall of Fame in 1936. He was one of the best all-around players in the history of baseball.

Babe Ruth (1895 - 1948)

Ruth was raised in a poverty-stricken environment. He was sent to a reform school when he was seven years old. He spent ten years in that institution.

Babe struck out 1,330 times.

Salk, American medical researcher. He developed the first vaccine against polio in 1952 using inactivated polio virus. Mass immunization programs were implemented using this newly developed vaccine.

Jonas Salk (1914 - 1995)

After graduating from Medical School in 1939, Salk applied to Mt. Sinai and The Rockefeller Institute but was turned down for employment at both institutions.

Despite countless attempts to cultivate a polio virus for a vaccine, intense opposition, skepticism, criticism, public fears and bad press, he never wavered in his belief that his vaccine would work. He worked eighteen hour days. After his first field trials of his new vaccine, he stated, "When you inoculate children with a polio vaccine, you don't sleep well for a number of nights."

Sartre, French novelist, playwright and philosopher. He was the foremost proponent of existentialism. His works include *The Roads to Freedom*, *Black Orpheus*, *Being and Nothingness*.

Jean-Paul Sartre (1905 - 1980)

Sartre's father died shortly after his birth. He was raised by his maternal grandparents. Jean was small for his age. Other children would not play with him because they considered him so odd and so different. He spelled poorly and did not do well in school. He was ten years old before he completed a year in school.

Schubert, Austrian romantic composer. He wrote over 600 songs. In one year, he composed 5 operas, 2 symphonies, 2 masses, and 146 songs. Works include *Ave Maria*, *Unfinished* Symphony.

Franz Schubert (1797 - 1828)

Schubert was one of eighteen children. His family lived in poverty. Only through the help of generous and devoted friends was he able to survive and obtain the necessary supplies to write his music. He was largely unappreciated during his lifetime.

Hark, Hark, the Lark was written down on the back of a menu in a tavern. He died at age thirty-one.

Sewell, British novelist. Her single novel was *Black Beauty*, published in 1877.

Anna Sewell (1820 - 1878)

Anna was crippled at a young age and lived with tremendous pain most of her life. A childhood accident prevented her from running and playing. She had to stay in bed for long periods of time.

At age fifty-one, she was no longer able to stand. She was physically confined to her home. She wanted to do something worthwhile before she died. She decided to write a story about a horse. It took her six years to finish her story. Many days she was too sick to write. Her book, *Black Beauty*, was published in 1877. A year later she died.

Sinclair, American novelist and social reformer. His works include *The Jungle, The Metropolis, King Coal, Dragon's Teeth.*

Upton Sinclair (1878 - 1968)

Sinclair's father was an alcoholic. Upton began supporting his parents at age thirteen. His mother disapproved of his writings.

Sinclair was paid only $1,000 for his first five novels. He ran unsuccessfully in California for the United States House of Representatives, the Senate, and the Governorship.

Skelton, American comedian and pantomimist. His career spanned vaudeville to television

Red Skelton (1913 -)

Red Skelton grew up in extreme poverty. His father died from alcoholism two months before Red was born. His brothers abused him. On one occasion, they almost drowned him. Once they dragged him, tied behind a motorcycle. Red slept in an attic infested with rats. Often, there was little for his family to eat.

Skelton's adult life was also filled with tragedy. His only son died from leukemia at a young age. His second wife committed suicide. Skelton lived a sad and lonely life while giving the world laughter.

Tillich, German-American theologian and philosopher. His works include *The Courage to Be*, *Dynamics of Faith*, *Systematic Theology*. He tried to relate Christian faith to the problems of human living.

Paul Tillich (1886 - 1965)

Tillich was plagued by depression throughout his life.

Tolstoy, Russian novelist and philosopher. He advocated non-violence and a simple life. His works include *War & Peace*, *Anna Karenina*, *Childhood, Boyhood and Youth*, *The Death of Ivan Ilyich*.

Leo Tolstoy (1828 - 1910)

Tolstoy's mother died when he was two years old. His father died when he was nine years old. His aunt became his legal guardian. She died when he was thirteen years old. He was a small, unattractive boy who was very self-conscious about his appearance. When he was a teenager, his tutor exclaimed, "Leo neither will nor can study." He was a "gifted nonachiever" until college. He quit law school at the University of Moscow to pursue his interest in philosophy.

Toulouse-Lautrec, French painter, graphic artist. He was an extremely productive artist.

Henri de Toulouse-Lautrec
(1864 - 1901)

Lautrec was only four feet tall. The growth of his legs were stunted when he broke them at age fourteen. His famous series, *The Circus*, was painted while he was in an insane asylum following a nervous breakdown. His paintings and lithographs received little attention during his lifetime.

Truman, Thirty-second President of the United States.

Harry Truman (1884 - 1972)

As a child, Truman was very accident prone and sickly. At age nine, he was paralyzed for a short time after contracting diphtheria. He was very nearsighted and wore thick glasses.

Truman never went to college. He was rejected as a candidate for West Point because of poor eyesight. He went into the men's clothing business in 1919 in Kansas City. This business failed three years later. He worked at a number of jobs before entering politics.

Truman was content with serving in the Senate. He never aspired to the presidency.

Van Gogh, Dutch painter and draftsman. One of the first Expressionists. He produced more than two hundred works.

Vincent Van Gogh (1853 - 1890)

Van Gogh failed the entrance exams to the Seminary. He was dismissed from his lay preacher missionary work at the age of twenty-seven. He lived in solitude and poverty throughout most of his life. He sold only one of his paintings during his lifetime.

Wallace, American author. Other works include: *The Boyhood of Christ*, *The Wooing of Malkaton*.

Lew Wallace (1827 - 1905)

When he began his famous book, *Ben Hur*, *A Tale of the Christ*, Wallace did not hold any strong religious convictions. He started the book to learn about Christ and to decide for himself about particular religious truths. He worked on the book for seven years, writing in his spare time. As he was completing his book, he was in constant danger. He was the Governor of the Territory of New Mexico and Billy the Kid threatened to kill him.

Washington, B., American educator. Built and headed the Tuskegee Institute. He was an advocate for vocational education.

Booker T. Washington (1856 - 1915)

Booker T. Washington was born a slave on a plantation. He was raised in poverty, lacking the necessities of life, and without any opportunities for an education. He knew very little about his mother and nothing about his father.

Washington G., First President of the United States, called the "Father of His Country."

George Washington (1732-1799)

Washington's father died before George was twelve years old. He lived temporarily with various relatives and was eventually taken in by his half brother. George had little formal schooling. He learned map making and surveying on his own. George married a young widow and helped raise her children.

Washington led a small, weak, untrained and unequipped army of patriots through harsh and difficult times against a well-trained, well-equipped and well-organized British Army. This was his first experience commanding such a large army.

Whitman, American poet, essayist.

Walt Whitman (1819 - 1892)

Whitman worked hard in Washington hospitals during the Civil War. He developed paralysis as a result of this strenuous work.

When *Leaves of Grass* was published in 1855, critics rejected his form and content, branding Whitman with a life-long unsavory reputation. Whitman frequently revised and added to this collection of poems for over thirty-five years.

Your Name Birthdate

What have been your major obstacles?

What have you accomplished?

Your Hero

Dates: Birth-Death

What did this person overcome?

What did this person accomplish?

"Acceptance of what has happened is the first step to overcoming the consequences of any misfortune."

William James

"You have to accept whatever comes and the only important thing is that you meet it with the best you have to give."

Eleanor Roosevelt

"He that can't endure the bad, will not live to see the good."

Jewish Proverb

"My strength lies solely in my tenacity."

Louis Pasteur

"It's not what you have lost but what you have left that counts."

Harold Russell

"Know how sublime it is to suffer and be strong."

Henry Wadsworth Longfellow

"Let us live then and be glad."

Anonymous

"You may have a fresh start any moment you choose, for this thing that we call failure is not the falling down, but the staying down."

Mary Pickford

About the Author

Steven Kaelin, M.S. has worked with children and families in a variety of educational and counseling settings for over twenty years. He has designed and conducted parent training workshops throughout Utah and Nevada.

Steven has a Master's degree in Educational Psychology from the University of Utah. He is presently the Parent Training Coordinator for the Utah Division of Child and Family Services. He is married and is the father of two children.